MAKING MONEY ONLINE

As a Writing Retiree

ANYWAY

Despite

1-STAR REVIEWS

Internet Business Ideas PART II

PEGGY HATCHET

MAKING MONEY ONLINE AS A WRITING RETIREE

Copyright © 2016 by Peggy Hatchet

All rights reserved.

ISBN: 13: 978-1535479813
ISBN-10: 1535479817

TABLE OF CONTENTS

THANK YOU	**9**
SECTION I	**11**
DON'T DWELL ON THE 1-STAR REVIEW	**12**
THE WRITER'S BLOCK	**13**
CREATIVE BALANCE	**18**
SCHEDULING UNINTERRUPTED WRITING TIME	**20**
LEARNING FROM GREAT WRITING ACHIEVERS	**24**
UNEDUCATED AUTHORS	25
AUTHORS WHO HAD NO FORMAL TRAINING	**27**
HOW TO BECOME THE BEST WRITER YOU CAN BE	**29**
ANALYZED QUOTES	**34**
SHOULD WRITERS PREPARE FOR CRITICISM?	**37**
SECTION II	**40**

WHAT THE HELL ARE YOU TRYING TO SAY?	41
SHUT UP AND SUCK IT UP	43
WHAT'S SO SPECIAL ABOUT OTHER AUTHORS?	46
TAKING ADVICE FROM OTHER WRITERS	50

CLICHÉS — 53

CLICHÉS AND THE MODERN SCRIBE	54

SECTION III — 74

BEAUTIFUL WORDS FOR YOUR CREATIVE WRITING VOCABULARY THAT REPRESENT EXQUISITENESS	75
OTHER WORDS FOR YOUR CREATIVE VOCABULARY THAT REPRESENT UNPLEASANTNESS OR DESPAIR	79
FRENCH WORDS AND PHRASES FOR YOUR VAIN, CONCEITED OR ROMANTIC CHARACTER	81
PAYING WRITING OPPORTUNITIES FOR THE RETIREE	86
FREELANCE WRITING PROSPECTS THAT PAY WELL	90
ONLINE SITES WRITERS FIND INTERESTING	92

BONUS SECTION — 95

NON-INTERNET HOME BUSINESS IDEAS	96
3 BUSINESSES THAT DAY-JOB WORKERS CAN START	105
WAYS AND MEANS TO MAKE MONEY ONLINE	107
FREELANCING	107
AFFILIATE MARKETING	109
ARTS, CRAFTS & SEWN ITEMS	111

AVOID "CONTENT WRITING MILLS" — 112

VIDEO MARKETING	113
Q & A (EXPERTISE)	114
GET PAID TO WRITE FAMILY & PARENTING ARTICLES	**116**
GET PAID TO WRITE ESSAYS	**118**
I CAN'T AFFORD TO GIVE A DAMN WHAT YOU THINK	**120**

SECTION IV   123

WRITING THIS BOOK DID ME ALL THE GOOD   **124**

Thank You

To Maggie, Ellen, Micah, Lemuel, Faye and others who emailed me to ask for "more".

Lotsa' love and well wishes,

Peggy

I couldn't write freely without the understanding of those in my house. I'm fortunate to have you; and therefore, grateful.

SECTION I
You, the Writer

Don't Dwell on the 1-Star Review

"If you write (or paint or dance or sculpt or sing), someone will try to make you feel lousy about it..."
                                                    --Stephen King

Writing is mystical. Influential. Eternal.
Every human writes, but few do it well enough for it to matter. However, in their early stages of writing, rejection taunted even the "few".

Breaking into the big leagues of your career choice means you have to get past the *gatekeepers*. You have scoffers, bystanders and blockers who are literally *in the way*-- on purpose. Some are envious. Others are just plain irritating by design.

When you encounter them, keep moving. Don't slow down to talk about their pettiness. And by all means, don't embrace the negativity.

1-star reviews come with writing. Malicious comments are confidence-killers designed to do just that. Writers cannot afford to give a damn-- so don't.

...lest the writer in you die.

"Talent is helpful in writing, but guts are absolutely necessary."-- Jessamyn West

The Writer's Block

Whether you're a seasoned writer or a casual freelancer, you're sure to experience *'blocks'* to your creative flow. It's when you can't think; your ideas stop moving freely and you might walk away from the project indefinitely.

Blocks to the creative experience occur for a number of reasons, none of which are exclusive to one or all writers. Triggers vary.

Most of us already know *why* we can't write. And we're usually too frustrated to *see* the solution. At the root of most blocks is a literary gnat buzzing around in your thinking space, telling you "you'll never be good enough to earn a decent living at it."

It's easy to slip into this oblivion after the rejection of a piece that you *put a lot into*. It's natural process for writers to put a lot into their writing. That's not the problem. We have to learn to take a lot out, after putting it in. That's the problem.

We must also understand that though basic writing is common to everyone, not everyone has the ability of creative flow. The ability to write best-sellers. Creative flow separates the novelist from the signer of credit card receipts or the one filling out applications on a job search.

Creative flow distinguishes between writers, quality being the determinant, which-- as in every profession, creates the resentment that comes with competition. Even among competent peers and colleagues, there is an unethical undertone of book-bashing chatter that's intended to undermine the author as well as the work. This is a block indeed-- if you allow it.

I'll repeat. Writers cannot afford to give a damn about a 1-star rating accompanied by an ill-intended comment. You can't control what others say or do. But you *can* control how you respond. And that's power belonging only to *you*.

"I don't give a damn!" I said.

"That's a stupid response." my friend said.

"That's your opinion." I said.

"How can you be so dismissive about someone rating your book with one star and then saying mean stuff on top of it? I don't get it." she said. "They dismissed your book in the comments as *nothing to waste time on*."

"The way I see it, I can use my time and energy one of two ways on this issue." I said. "I can waste it trying to figure out why someone wrote nasty comments; or I can choose not to give a damn. So I choose to shrug it off and not give a damn."

"Are you saying it doesn't bother you at all?" she asked.

"When you first brought it to my attention, I felt all kinds of ways. Shocked, pissed off and indignant. Then I realized. The person giving the

1-star rating and who proceeded to make a dismissive comment chose to exercise their power in that manner, however disagreeable. In my own way, I chose to do the same." I explained.

"You're not making any sense." she said.

"Okay. What would you do?" I asked.

"I would go online and give them a piece of my mind. You can't let people get away with doing things like that. They'll keep doing it." she said.

"If I knew the person who said this, yes, I would have a conversation with them." I said. "But this Internet person could be anyone. I'm not interested in having a back-and-forth with someone I don't know, who doesn't matter. I don't give a damn what they write. I can't afford to. Therefore, I don't."

"Any other time you would deal with it." she said.

"I *am* dealing with it-- just not the way you want me to." I said. "The best way to deal with negative people (the ones you know and don't know) is to *not* deal with them. Let them take their own poison." I said.

"Well, you're a better person than I am. I would be raising holy hell if somebody said that about my book." she said.

"Yeah and all you would get for it is high blood pressure, with veins popping out of your temple and maybe even a stroke." I joked.

We ended the conversation on that light note. Both of us remained steadfast in our positions. I'm happy not giving a damn.

Getting someone out of your head is the hardest thing to do, once you let them in. And all writers know that their *headspace* is off limits to everyone but characters.

MAKING MONEY ONLINE AS A WRITING RETIREE

Creative Balance

Creative balance (in writing) is when every aspect of your process is in harmony with your efforts. It's when your writing space is clutter-free; there's no noise or distraction; you have no other issues pressing on your mind. In other words, your mental passage is clear. Words and ideas are cohesive and free-flowing.

Imagination is vital to all forms of writing. For character-based novels, imagination gives life and purpose to the storyline. No imagination, no fictional narrative.

My routine for sustaining a clear creative path is simple enough. It's hard to maintain sometimes. Discipline is the main virtue, but writing is useless without dedication and consistency.

Normally, writers work at home. When I have to research a subject, I write quite a bit at the library. Otherwise, my writing is done at home.

I treat my home-writing process like my former day job, in terms of keeping a schedule. I rise early; groom and dress; have light nourishment; and do light chores, such as make the bed, prayer and meditation, for instance.

My morning routine takes about an hour to an hour and a half. I rise at 4:30 or 5 a.m.; take an hour to an hour and a half to organize part of the day; and by 6:00 or 6:30 a.m., I'm ready to write.

There's no TV blaring or radio noise. Sometimes I play low-volume classical music. It relaxes me. Some say it frees pent-up creativity. I can't say if it does that. But classical music is definitely relaxing.

If I don't turn the phone ringer off, I lose creative flow each time it rings. Those I've talked to agree that silencing their phone is difficult to do. Talking on the phone is an impulse, a thing we do because we believe we're *supposed* to. It's a habit.

Adjusting to *some* changes is harder than adapting to others; and "it will take some doing," as my mother would say.

Anything we do instinctively is a *habit*. Habits aren't bad, when they're good.

Talking on the phone for long periods, usually about nothing constructive, is a habit for most of us-- a wasteful and unproductive habit.

Unproductive habits are the hardest to break, because we get so much pleasure from them. However, breaking them is worth every effort.

The good news is you don't suffer any physical withdrawal symptoms, when breaking the phone habit.

Giggles.

Scheduling Uninterrupted Writing Time

I mentioned earlier that I get up at 4:30 or 5 a.m. and am ready to write by six. *Scheduling,* in other words, balances the day and adds quality to what has to be done.

For example, secular jobs require *organizational thinking*. You get up at a scheduled time; groom yourself; have a light breakfast; and off to work you go. Organized, right?

In contrast, let's say my day begins with no structure. I would probably wake up and *not get up*. I'd have my laptop, notebooks and pieces of paper strewn across my crumpled bed. Lounging around in my peejays all day would be the norm.

My hair would be unkempt, my teeth unbrushed and my bed unmade. I would jump up when it's time for the husband and kids to be home from their respective places. *Don't make that face; you know it's true.*

I would have to pretend that I've been productive; making up a story about "running errands" or taking care of other "important business" outside the home. Living a lie is not as simple as it appears. It takes work-- and yes, *organization*.

Not only would creativity have a block, but also self-worth and self-esteem would go into shock.

Imbalance is easy to fall victim to, when

working from home-- *working* being the operative word. You might say an unorganized day is a day *missed* from work.

Writers thrive on organization. Organized schedules organized personal care and organized working atmosphere equal *organized thoughts* and freely drawn-upon imagination. A writer needs this discipline in order to write, *unblocked*.

Here's an example of a schedule to give you an idea of how you can plan your day around your writing. Times and activities should reflect personal requirements, as it relates to your individual home life and responsibility.

Time	Activity
4:30 a.m. 5:00 a.m.	Get up; shower; change; make bed; light breakfast; de-clutter work space
6 or 6:30	Write; go to work
9:00 a.m.	Take a break; plan lunch menu; get dinner started; take five minutes outside; breathe
10: a.m.	read over and correct what I've written; write some more
12 noon	have a light lunch; finish preparing dinner
1 p.m.	Change bed linen; Put towels & linen in washer; dust
2 p.m.	Take towels & linen from dryer; fold and put them away
2:30 p.m.	water plants, read a book, relax, etc.

Setting a timer or an alarm clock (whichever is appropriate) for each block of time maintains a fluid schedule. Writing can be all-consuming. Hours will pass and leave you wondering where the time went. With an alarm, time can work *for you.*

Likewise, regular day jobs have designated times for *breaks* and *lunch,* breaking the day into segments. Since you're already familiar with the organization that comes with a day job, it wouldn't be difficult to adopt it for your writing time at home. You can ease right into it.

Having a schedule also frees up the space that *worrying* would otherwise occupy. *"I have to get up. I don't know what's for dinner. I need to wash dishes. The floor needs vacuuming. Blah, blah and blah"*

The focus is to develop an organized ritual that fits within your lifestyle as a retiree. Or maybe you're a working person with a spouse and kids. However, retirees are in a better position than most.

While remembering that not all solutions work for all writers, most of us tend to mismanage common sense methods -- dismissing them as mere *'common sense'* directives. Ironic.

We take *common sense* knowledge for granted, demeaning it as irrelevant. However, I submit to you that not everyone has or uses common sense, which makes *all* knowledge relevant, at all times.

Your writing is only as good as your organization. Removing the clutter of disorganization removes most or all writer's block,

depending on whether *organization* is your only problem.

If there's a gnat buzzing in your head because of negative feedback or self-doubt, you have to get rid of it. Otherwise, writing-- for you will be a distant desire.

Learning from Great Writing Achievers

"When you wanna learn how to do something, ask someone who's mastered it." This is my position. If you want to know what motivates inventors, read their biographies, to get understanding of their mindset and mannerisms.

Likewise, writers seeking to publish great novels and other useful books will study the life of masterful authors. You will find that some of our great writers emerged from distress so traumatic that it often interrupted their education.

Fortunately, they didn't need an English degree or any special training to write successfully. They simply had a love for reading and writing.

To this point, quite a few famous authors have no academic training. In some cases, their plight left them barely finishing high school.

DO NOT read this as an anti-education proposal. That's not what this is. I'm merely saying that *"Not having a formal education doesn't justify abandoning your writing dreams."*

If you desire an education, get one, no matter your age. However, if you don't have one, and are succeeding without it, well… there you have it.

As for famous authors who have little or no formal education, their success is proof that you can live your dream without it, when situations and circumstances say you have to.

Uneducated Authors

Apparently, these authors inadvertently used their traumatic childhood experiences to fortify their written word.

Remember. Accomplished authors are ordinary people. They have vices; they have love affairs; they are married with kids; and some of them are divorced with drinking problems.

The point is to find a connection to their struggle, as well as to their success. This helps you realize that you can master your craft, despite your hardships.

As a retiree who writes for a living (and who has no formal training, by the way), I refer to the struggle aspect because of a natural association.

Retirees have the most important commodity that a writer needs --free *time*. Writers blossom with free, uninterrupted time. The writers I know would love to have the time they need to flow in their creativity. But most of them are full-time employees. Having been one, I understand.

On the other hand, retirees are no longer obligated to an employee's work schedule. They can create their own. No more "wishing for time to do some of the things" you like doing. Now you have it. Decide what you're going to do with it.

Retirees with a passion for writing are especially fortunate to have free time, as there's nothing to hinder them from their work.

Nevertheless, when *free time* replaces the ease of organization, it's common to fall into creative *imbalance* and *disarray*.

Being retired doesn't mean you should start preparing for the grave; or that your days are now empty and useless.

In fact, when you retire, life relaxes to the point that you *can* now see things you were otherwise too busy to notice.

Learning about the struggles and the triumphs of well-known authors is fundamental to shaping your own writing journey.

You will be able to overcome your own obstacles without personal condemnation when you know and understand how other prominent authors successfully conquered similar ones.

Keep in mind that their example serves only as encouragement. Regardless of similarities in life circumstances, your experience is unique to *your* journey. Their life's example merely shows you that your writing goal is reachable.

Authors Who Had No Formal Training

William Faulkner

Faulkner is a Nobel Prize winner, who never earned a high school diploma. He enrolled in the University of Mississippi, dropping out after three semesters.

Charles Dickens
One of eight children from an impoverished family whose father was thrown into debtor's prison when he was a boy, Dickens had little and patchy education. He wrote many great novels.

Ray Bradbury
Bradbury said he "didn't believe in colleges". Therefore, he barely finished high school and never attended college, though his book *Fahrenheit 451* is required reading in many high schools.

Truman Capote
Truman had a traumatic childhood, often abandoned by his parents. He was 41 when he published his nonfiction novel *In Cold Blood*.

Maya Angelou

Suffering sexual abuse and racial discrimination, Angelou experienced emotional shock that left her mute for five years. She gave birth to her son three weeks after graduating high school. Working as a pimp and prostitute, being unable to attend college and desperate for money, her friend James Baldwin encouraged her to publish her now famous autobiography *I Know Why the Caged Bird Sings*.

Mark Twain

Samuel Langhorne Clemens had to drop out of school at age 12 and work for food and rations after his father died. Like Bradbury, he educated himself in public libraries. Well into his 30s, he reinvented himself as a writer, using his work as a boat pilot to provide his new identity, *Mark Twain* (steamboat slang for measuring two fathoms).

H. G. Wells

A leg injury left eight-year-old Wells bedridden. Despite dropping out of school with the affliction, Wells became a science fiction novelist known for *The War of the Worlds* and *The Time Machine*.

How to Become the Best Writer You Can Be

The idea of *rating is over-rated*. I wanted to get that point out first. Rating is overrated. I've read books with five-star rating and sat disappointed that it didn't measure up to its so-called "rating".

Likewise, out of curiosity, I dared to part the pages of a low-rated book and came away pleasantly surprised, fulfilled and gratified that I wasn't deterred by the so-called "ranking".

Receiving a one-star rating is not as bad as having written one-star material. The difference is clear.

Now we can move on.

When someone rates your work below the line of what's considered "good", you might question whether you're *author* material. We often look at writing through a single lens. Writing is multi-dimensional. In fact, there are thousands-- even millions of writers, but few great authors.

Though some people make it their mission to discredit others, it's also possible their criticism has merit and can therefore be helpful. What does it mean when a reader under-rates your book? It can only mean one of two things. Either the assessment is true or the reader has unresolved issues. Which ever it turns out to be, writers *absolutely must be* resilient to survive the pettiness of competition, if they are to enjoy writing as a career.

The principal concern in this is your response to "rating slash criticism". Will criticism of your book make you bitter or better? Keep in mind that everyone will not relate to your message. And that's okay. I'll take a few million satisfied readers out of the billions of people on our planet.

"...only he is an emancipated thinker who is not afraid to write foolish things." --**Anton Chekhov**

Writers must constantly evolve into greater thoughts and freshly imagined demonstration. What reads *foolishly* to some reads *marvelously* to others.

Did you know that Stephen King's books earn him an estimated 17 million annually? Hollywood made movies from his books because of the "foolishness" of them. King was not afraid to use the content of his imagination, no matter how weird it appeared to others. However, he didn't start out that way.

In his memoir, *"On Writing"*, he talks in raw terms about writing.

"I can't lie and say there are no bad writers. Sorry, but there are lots of bad writers," King writes.

We don't need Stephen King or Toni Morrison or Willa Cather to tell us that *bad writers* exist. What

we *do* need is not to be one of them. There are no bad stories, just bad storytellers.

King says television is "poisonous to creativity". While most people understand this fact, some don't see the harm in having a TV blaring in the room while they struggle to write. It's madness.

Writers have to look inward, to their imagination, to produce fascinating books. Watching TV cripples the ability to dream, to invent and to create.

Imagine an electronic device watching you constantly; telling you what to think, what to believe, what to eat and how to feel. That's the relationship you have with your TV. You are actually engaging in a one-way conversation. It's talking to you, but can't hear or respond to anything you say-- not a good scenario.

In his book, King says "If you want to be a writer, you must do two things above all others: **read a lot** and **write a lot**."

Depending on your writing genre and the age range you write for, I believe it also matters *"what"* you read.

For example, if a person reads only trashy and vulgar material, they'll write tasteless books. It can't come out, if it doesn't go in, right?

Individuals who love reading romance novels will likely write in that genre. Likewise, reading murder mysteries is the pathway to learning how to write thrillers.

Conversely, one does not always write in genres related to what one reads. A varied reading library returns diversity in writing. I consider myself a multi-genre writer, for instance-- because I read a variety of books, novels, literature, journals, periodicals and so forth that broaden imaginative reach and expand knowledge.

Writing is universal; but effectively great writing resides on a distant paradise, waiting for the audacious writer to discover it.

Each writer has to find his or her own way, despite what others suggest.

Rudeness must be the least of a writer's (or potentially great writer's) concerns. Some will behave outlandishly toward your work, for no other reason except that *they can*.

Earlier in his career, King received letters calling him murderous, a bigot, homophobic, and even psychopathic, often making him ashamed of what he wrote.

At age 40, he realized that there would always be a naysayer, who knows nothing else, except to accuse great writers of being a *waste of talent*. He writes, "If you disapprove, I can only shrug my shoulders. It's what I have."

Sitting behind a computer and surfing for something or someone to criticize and disagree with is easy to do. All you have to do is sit on your miserable tush and decide "who" the next target is. I say, *"Whatever floats your sinking boat, have at it."*

However, writing, editing and gathering the courage to publish a book is the real work. Even

when a publisher rejects your 500-page novel, at least you were able to pull 500 pages of imagination out of your mind and organize it into a book. That's a major accomplishment. Don't wait for the "pat on the back". Pat yourself on the back.

You have to know that you did something great and noteworthy, whether it makes the best-seller list or not.

If you've published a book, applaud your efforts. If you're "under-rated", so what?

Rating is overrated. How you rate yourself is all that matters.

Analyzed Quotes

"Cut out all those exclamation marks. An exclamation mark is like laughing at your own joke." --F. Scott Fitzgerald

Though we recognize Fitzgerald as one of the great writers of the century, I disagree with this notion to a degree.

Exclamation points are necessary on those occasions when nothing else can convey the mood of the moment. If a character is shouting, excited, or frightened, an exclamation point is the only way to portray that emotion.

"The ability of writers to imagine what is not the self, to familiarize the strange and mystify the familiar, is the test of their power." --Toni Morrison

This is the result of creative flow-- the ability to imagine opposite realities for each actuality. To tell a story in a way that makes the stranger feel at home and the friend alienated is masterful.

"When you can't create, you can work." --Henry Miller

This is true. At one time, I thought each day of writing had to produce this wonderful storyline essence. And when I couldn't do that, it meant I shouldn't write that day. However, I learned that I could still do writing *work* by reading over what I had already written and making corrections as I

found mistakes. This way, I never waste a day of writing (*work*).

"I try to leave out the parts that people skip." --Elmore Leonard.

For me, this would require reading, reading and more reading of the manuscript, trying to find the parts that bore me. I have removed sentences that didn't' belong. However, it wasn't a novel or anything like that. The trouble with *removing* is that most writers believe all of their writing is relevant. Getting rid of parts of it is like amputating a limb.

"There is nothing to writing. All you do is sit down at a typewriter and bleed." --Ernest Hemingway

Perhaps what he's saying is that for an author, writing is your life's blood. In the writing process, the words are metaphorically "written in blood". It also helps to know when you need a *transfusion*.

"Abandon the idea that you are going to finish. Lose track of the 400 pages and write just one page for each day, it helps. Then when it gets finished, you are always surprised." --John Steinbeck

This would require more effort for me, and probably for most. It's difficult not to think forward to the *finished* work. But I guess it's an acquired discipline-- perhaps even beneficial.

"Every great and original writer, in proportion a he is great and original, must himself create the taste by which he is to be relished." --William Wordsworth

Readers recognize an original writer's style and can spot it anywhere. They develop a *taste* for *that* essence, *that* originality from *that* author. Such is the case with all great writers. Their writing style has a flavour all its own. No one can imitate it. They can only relish it.

Should Writers Prepare for Criticism?

The answer is *"yes"*.

"If you write (or paint or dance or sculpt or sing, I suppose), someone will try to make you feel lousy about it..." King writes.

We've already established that some people make a mission of tearing others down. The beauty of it lies in the fact that no one can tear you down, unless you give them permission.

So make up your mind that the few naysayers' opinions are of no consequence. If you're true to your imagination and allow no one to dictate what you should write; and if what you write serves a purpose, the universe makes room for that which embodies good will-- be it fiction or non-fiction.

Since outside forces can't harm you unless you permit them, you must secure your own thinking. Every worthwhile endeavour is a blend of consistency, trial and error. Success doesn't come ready-made. We roll up our sleeves, endure the many scrapes and bruises of the trade and remain consistent through it all.

Afterwards, and on the other side of success, we realize that the *extra* struggle we endured wasn't necessary at all. We only needed to love ourselves and to believe in ourselves.

To do that, an individual would have to avoid naysayers and confidence killers. Keep a positive mind and work at your trade *your* way. Anybody can sit on the sidelines and dole out instructions, but the test lies in doing the actual work.

You have to remain positive even when you perceive failure in your attempts. Never doubt yourself to the point of destruction. Many die broken because of this.

King believes, "Optimism is a perfectly legitimate response to failure." --if, indeed, *it is* failure.

One other thing King said resonates with me, on mastering description, as it relates to effective writing. He said, "Descriptions begin in the writer's imagination, but should finish in the reader's."

Character descriptions and all other storyline segments are important to the reader's experience. Good writers paint pictures with their words.

The reader is also able to smell fragrances, feel the gentle touch of a hand or the coolness of a breeze; see beautiful sights and hear all associated sounds.

In other words, a skilful writer visualizes what he or she wants the reader to experience, and then translates their vision onto paper in the form of written descriptions.

King says he describes things "in a way that causes his readers to prickle with recognition."

We began this segment encouraging writers to prepare for criticism, as a means of protecting their headspace against it-- not from a place of dread.

The message in that is *people can't tear you down, unless you give them permission.*

SECTION II
Imagination and Process

What the Hell Are You Trying to Say?

Have you ever written or read a novel where the writing goes on and on about a matter? We think because we write seven hundred pages that they're all worth reading. No. Sometimes, maybe. But most of the time, *no*. And we have the gall to be upset that no one wants to *read* the seven hundred pages--two hundred of which are boring.

There's an audience for books that have a gazillion pages. I like reading biographies and autobiographies, historical accounts, great literature and such. Most of these have three hundred or more pages.

Technology has now made it possible for us to take information in blocks, passages of thought on handheld devices. Writers are adjusting. They're writing to master the *gadget* transition.

Figure out what the hell you're trying to say, and then say it-- minus the extra frills.

Good writing lends so many thrilling aspects to reading. Whether we read fiction, how-to manuals, romance novels or a gripping biography, we are enriched by part or all of its content. It's all in how the writer says what he or she has to say.

What we can imagine is often wonderful, as it pertains to storytelling. Translating that wonder into *condensed* written word, and not losing its essence, requires artistry and skill.

It's not practical to insert every thought you have into a plot, no matter how compelling. Each concept has to do more than just sound good *to you*. It has to fit in with, if not enhance, the entire narrative.

Saying *everything* is not necessary-- or sensible.

Shut Up and Suck it Up

Writers of books must find their way past being *touchy* about editing. We have to be able to say "goodbye" to sentences that don't work in the story.

Sometimes we have to just *'shut up and suck it up'*.

Keeping a notebook nearby is good for writing down those sentences that you *can't seem to throw away.* Maybe you can use them in a future project.

Writing is not a contest of intellect-- or of big, rarely used words. Writing is a masterful presentation of imagined scenarios transferred to print, in true-to-life sequence.

Readers gravitate to authors who write on subjects that they know about, including life experience. Authenticity lasts. It's timeless. Classic. Nobel prizes are awarded to authors who are able to relate genuine visions through artistry of words.

To the writer, *all* of his or her written words are relevant. They're like newborn babies that you're nurturing. You fuss over them.

However, to the reader, some of those words are irrelevant, redundant or altogether confusing.

What writer will view parts of their work as *'irrelevant'* and *'redundant'*? Answer: the serious one.

Serious writers don't like it, but they understand they have to *cut* out unneeded stuff, *shut up* the run-on conversations and *suck it up* when these issues are pointed out. By doing so, he or she can figure out *what the hell* they're trying to say.

Is it possible for readers to prefer a seventy-page booklet to a four-hundred-page novel? Yes. Does this mean writers should restrict themselves to writing short-reads? Of course not.

This simply means every writer should know or figure out what they're trying to say, and then say it-- no more, no less.

When writers convey clearly and precisely, it won't matter if the book is sixty pages or a thousand. Readers have an appetite for meaningful substance. Stories or information that enhances their thinking or world view in an area.

Does the book perform well? Does it do what you want it to do? Does it answer a question or serve a valuable purpose?

Successful books leave the reader informed, inspired and less indifferent. Fiction or non-fiction, a book's content will distinguish it-- not its length. Being able to skillfully combine content with lengthiness is surely a work of excellence.

The point is: knowing what you're trying to say and being unafraid to say it exactly how you want to say it. If you give the world eighty pages, make each page relevant; and the same for a five-hundred-page novel.

It's easy to confuse length with substance, thinking many pages means the writer has a lot of knowledge.

Writers ultimately grow past their mistakes. Having them pointed out is the grueling part.

Nevertheless, never stop writing. Despite the criticism, never stop. Persistence breeds greatness.

What's So Special about Other Authors?

Imagine a person offering you advice on honouring marriage vows, but they've been married and divorced five times.

How will that work? No shade, but who wants to hear about honouring marriage vows from someone who possibly dishonoured theirs five times?

Just as you wouldn't think much of someone with short breath giving you running lessons, you wouldn't want an illiterate person's advice on how to master speed-reading for college exams.

Many established authors offer practical, no nonsense advice.

While no one follows their own rules 100% of the time, at least knowing what those rules are is half the responsibility. In fact, in a society where lawlessness is a growing trend, self-discipline, is an impressive virtue.

Daniel Baylis, author of *"The Traveler: Notes from an Imperfect Journey Around the World"*, wrote:

> "Writing is tough work. If I may be so bold as to attempt a smile, I'd say that it's like walking through a dark forest, but with your legs tied together."

Other authors wrote reflective short-takes that make sound literary sense. Look at these quotes, for instance:

"A bird doesn't sing because it has an answer; it sings because it has a song."--Maya Angelou

Many believe Angelou referred to her life in this statement, and deliberately phrased it to explain the title of her book, *"I Know Why the Caged Bird Sings"*. Nevertheless, the authentic wisdom of those words makes knowing "why" she wrote them irrelevant.

"I think perfection is ugly. Somewhere in the things humans make, I want to see scars, failure, disorder, distortion." --Yohji Yamamoto

This assertion clearly explains the writer's desire for realism and not fairy tale. You get a sense that he believes a 'flaw is evidence of human creativity'. *To err is human.* In other words, *flawlessness is imperfection,* and defects are evidence of one's *aim* for perfection, in terms of having brought a work to completion. Many great books lie rotting in dusty attics in musty boxes, because the disappointed writer left them unfinished.

"You are my idea of a good writer because you have an unmannered style, and when I read what you write, I hear you talking." --Isaac Asimov

A talented writer is able to speak on paper as though he or she is talking to you in person. A good writer is fearless and self-confident. They believe completely in their ability and is not afraid of someone disagreeing with what they write.

"Any project that's held up in general fear-based polishing is the victim of a crime. It's a crime because you're stealing that perfect work from a customer who will benefit from it. You're holding back the good stuff from the people who need it, afraid of what the people who don't will say." --Seth Godin

Writing is not an occupation for the "timid". And weak individuals, who care about what people say or think, will not survive the attempt. Timid and weak writers constantly deface their work, changing it, destroying it to please others. These sideline decriers wouldn't know good writing if they went on a date with it. But that's no deterrent to their insults.

Meanwhile, the people who are hungry for your original thought die of inspiration for lack of your imagination. Creative starvation is what it is.

Most writers held captive to this error are blinded to the reality of their own bondage. Great writers are not *people pleasers*. Likewise, people pleasers are not great writers.

"The worst enemy to creativity is self-doubt."
--Sylvia Plath

The self-doubt theory is self explanatory. If we are truthful, each of us has a story to tell of battles with self-doubt. It's common to life. Throughout your journey, you experience a lack of confidence as a result of doubting your abilities. This attitude is often the result of ridiculers belittling your work.

Scoffers can't harm you with their outside opinion. You can only harm yourself from the inside, your self-perception of who you are.

"Some writers enjoy writing, I am told. Not me. I enjoy having written." --George R.R. Martin

Remember when you would say, *'I'm writing a book,'* as though saying it would grant you the same notoriety, as though it were already published?

The finished work is always more gratifying than boasting of it being in the process. I bear witness.

We now have a glimpse of the wisdom that makes these authors who they are. I elaborated on them to impart what each citation said to me.

As such, observant writers can also benefit from these admissions. We learn and grow. No two writers are completely alike. However, the wisdom that guides success is timeless, universal.

Taking Advice from Other Writers

It's good to hear advice, and to read it. However, it's never healthy to embrace and try to implement all information labelled as *advice*.

Know *something* about the topic prior to asking someone's advice. At least you'll have a notion of what sounds right.

Famous authors paved a way for themselves through the competitive path of writing. They've paid their dues, and what they have to say about the art is important.

Nevertheless, their truth is not your truth or my truth. They can share it; it sounds good, even logical. However, each individual path is different, requiring measures unique to its standpoint.

Human paths start at the same juncture we call "birth". After that, they disperse into different directions, meeting up again at the intersection we call "death". Everything in between is different, individual, unique.

There's no rule that confines an author or writer into a box of conformed thinking. Allow no one, no so-called expert to belittle your written word. And never allow a scoffer the satisfaction of having weakened your power to create.

Humans tend to cling to the idea that they embrace, incorporating its value into their being.

Therefore, embrace nothing except the lessons of your own experience. Those, you can be certain of.

Over-seeking for advice is a sign of self-doubt, low self-esteem and no confidence in what you already know. Mostly we want to confirm what we know by seeing if anyone else views it the same way. And not finding agreement causes us to conform to a way that conflicts with our *'inner knowing'*.

You must write that which flows out of you. Writing the dictates of others technically makes you a transcriber, not an author.

Not the grocer, not the teacher, not the friend or the preacher's advice does a writer need.

Being afraid to be yourself and wanting to please others to the point of changing who you are is not healthy at any time-- and even more so for writers.

When you're not confident enough to be yourself, strong enough to stand on what comes out of you, you will embrace advice from anyone, as you try to find acceptance. *Self-acceptance* is what a writer needs. Accept yourself. Period.

Writing helps writers accept themselves. In some form, through characters, plots and the events we narrate, we tell part of our story; and we learn self-acceptance as a result.

Truth is the liberating element of writing. We add our truth in imaginative ways. And some of us are endowed with the magic of artfully speaking pure truth, which is a gift sparingly given.

The essence of advice is truth, although tainted sometimes by ill will and the stench of rivalry.

Advice is personal truth made of events encountered by the individual, while in pursuit of a goal or destination.

Motives and choices dictate the specifics of events that chastise or test the individual. This is what makes *advice* so suspect.

Writing is individual and unique, with an impartial perspective. It shares something eternal with the world. Be yourself. Be authentic. Be brave. Be the best writer you can be-- for you.

Everyone can write. But writing is *not* for everyone. Writing for the world takes nerves, guts, gallantry. You must speak the universal language.

Scrutiny is never as pervasive as when your written word reveals your soul to the world; and then another angry soul takes a sword to it-- cutting only themselves and blaming you for it.

MAKING MONEY ONLINE AS A WRITING RETIREE

CLICHÉS
What are they good for?

Clichés and the Modern Scribe

- ace in the hole
- ace up your sleeve
- acid test
- airing dirty laundry
- all in a day's work
- all talk, no action
- all booster, no payload
- all hat, no cattle
- all foam, no beer
- all hammer, no nail
- all icing, no cake
- all lime and salt, no tequila.
- all missile, no warhead
- all shot, no powder
- all sizzle, no steak
- all wax and no wick
- all that and a bag of chips
- all thumbs
- all wet
- all's fair in love and war
- almighty dollar
- always a bridesmaid
- ambulance chaser
- another day, another dollar
- ants in your pants
- apple-pie order
- arm and a leg

MAKING MONEY ONLINE AS A WRITING RETIREE

- armchair quarterback
- army brat
- art imitates life
- artsy-craftsy
- artsy-fartsy
- as luck would have it
- as old as time
- at loggerheads
- babe in the woods
- back against the wall
- back in the saddle
- back to square one
- back to the drawing board
- bad to the bone
- badge of honor
- ballpark figure
- balls to the wall
- baptism of fire
- bare bones
- bark is worse than the bite
- bark up the wrong tree
- bat out of hell
- bats in the belfry
- battle royal
- beat around the bush
- beat the bushes
- beats me
- behind the eight ball
- bent out of shape
- best foot forward
- bet your bottom dollar
- better half

- better late than never
- better mousetrap
- better safe than sorry
- better than ever
- better the Devil you know
- between a rock and a hard place
- beyond the pale
- bib and tucker
- big as life
- big fish in a small pond
- big man on campus
- (the) bigger they are
- bird in the hand

- birds and the bees
- birds of the feather
- bite the dust
- bite your tongue
- bitter disappointment
- black as coal
- blast from the past
- bleeding heart
- blind as a bat
- blood is thicker than water
- blood money
- blood on your hands
- blood sweat and tears
- blow this pop stand / joint
- blushing bride
- boil it down to
- bone of contention
- booze and broads
- bored to tears

- born and raised
- born with a silver spoon in your mouth
- born yesterday
- bottom line
- brain drain
- brain dump
- brass tacks
- bring home the bacon
- broken record
- brother's keeper (thy)
- bull by the horns
- bull in a china shop
- bump in the night
- busy as a bee
- but seriously
- by and large
- calm before the storm

- candle at both ends
- can't cut the mustard
- case of mistaken identity
- cat out of the bag
- cat got your tongue
- caught red-handed
- chapter and verse
- checkered career
- chickens come home to roost
- chomping at the bit
- cleanliness is next to godliness
- clear as a bell
- clear as mud
- cold shoulder

- communist conspiracy
- conniption fit
- could care less
- couldn't care less
- couldn't get to first base
- count your blessings
- countless hours
- creature comfort
- crime in the street
- curiosity killed the cat
- curry favor
- cut a fine figure
- cut and dried
- cut to the chase
- cut to the quick
- cute as a button
- darkest before the dawn
- dead as a doornail
- death and destruction
- death and taxes
- death's doorstep
- devil is in the details
- dim view
- dog days
- dog in the manger
- don't count your chickens before they're hatched
- don't do the crime if you can't do the time
- doubting Thomas
- down and dirty
- down in the dumps
- down pat

- down the drain/toilet
- down the hatch
- down to earth
- drive you up a wall
- Dutch uncle
- dyed in the wool
- E-ticket
- ear to the ground
- early bird catches the worm
- easier said than done
- easy as 1-2-3
- easy as pie
- eat crow
- eat humble pie
- enough already
- even money
- every dog has its day
- every fiber of my being
- everything but the kitchen sink
- evil twin
- existential angst
- experts agree
- eye for an eye
- facts of life
- fair-haired one
- fair weather friend
- fall off of a turnip truck
- fat slob
- favor us with a song
- fear and loathing
- feather your nest
- fellow traveler

- few and far between
- field this one
- fifteen minutes of fame
- fish nor fowl
- fly by night
- fly the coop
- for the birds
- fox in the henhouse
- Freudian slip
- fun and games
- fun in the sun
- garbage in, garbage out
- get the sack
- get your groove back
- gets my goat
- gift horse in the mouth
- gilding the lily
- give a damn
- give me a break
- gives me the creeps
- go him one better
- goes without saying
- good deed for the day
- good time was had by all
- Greek to me
- green thumb
- green-eyed monster
- grist for the mill
- guiding light
- hair of the dog
- hard to believe
- have a nice day

MAKING MONEY ONLINE AS A WRITING RETIREE

- head honcho
- heart's content
- hell-bent for leather
- hidden agenda
- high and the mighty (the)
- high on the hog
- hold a candle to
- hold your horses
- hold your tongue
- hook or by crook
- horse of a different color
- hot knife through butter
- how goes the battle?
- I beg to differ
- if the shoe fits
- I'm okay, you're okay
- in a nutshell
- in a pinch
- in a wink
- in harm's way
- in the tank
- in your dreams
- in your face
- inexorably drawn
- info dump
- influence peddling
- intents and purposes
- it was a dark and stormy night
- it won't fly
- Jack of all trades
- jockey for position
- Johnny-come-lately

- joined at the hip
- jump down your throat
- jump in with both feet
- jump on the bandwagon
- jump the gun
- jump her/his bones
- junk in the trunk
- jury is still out
- justice is blind
- keep an eye on you
- keep it down
- keep it simple, stupid
- keep up with the Joneses
- keep your cards close to vest
- keep your chin up
- keep your fingers crossed
- keep your powder dry
- kick ass
- kick butt
- kick the bucket
- kick up your heels
- kick you to the curb
- kick your feet up
- kid in a candy store
- kill two birds with one stone
- King's English
- king's ransom
- kiss and tell
- kiss ass
- kiss of death
- kit and caboodle
- knee-high to a grasshopper

MAKING MONEY ONLINE AS A WRITING RETIREE

- knock it out of the park
- knock on wood
- knock your socks off
- knocked up
- know him from Adam
- know the ropes
- know the score
- knuckle down
- knuckle sandwich
- knuckle under
- labor of love
- lap of luxury
- last but not least
- last-ditch effort
- last hurrah
- law of the jungle
- law of the land
- lay down the law
- leaps and bounds
- let sleeping dogs lie
- let the cat out of the bag
- let's split
- liberal media
- lie like a rug
- life and limb
- life imitates art
- life's a bitch
- lighten up
- lights out
- like a sore thumb
- like butter
- like the plague

- like there's no tomorrow
- lion's share
- litmus test
- little black book
- live and learn
- long and short of it
- long lost love
- look before you leap
- lounge lizard
- loved and lost
- low man on the totem pole
- luck of the draw
- luck of the Irish
- make my day
- male chauvinist
- man's best friend
- many moons
- many-splendored thing
- mark my words
- meaningful relationship
- mellow out
- moment of glory
- moment's respite
- Monday morning quarterback
- monkey suit
- monkey see, monkey do
- motherhood and apple pie
- movers and shakers
- moving experience
- my two cents
- neat as a pin
- needless to say

MAKING MONEY ONLINE AS A WRITING RETIREE

- nip it in the bud
- no guts, no glory
- no love lost
- no pain, no gain
- no stone unturned
- no time like the present
- nose to the grindstone
- not in my back yard
- not on your tintype
- number one fan
- numerous to mention
- off the wagon
- old college try
- old meets new
- older and wiser
- older than dirt
- older than Methuselah
- on the bandwagon
- on the nose
- on the wagon
- on thin ice
- one born every minute
- one foot in the grave
- one in a million
- only game in town
- only to be met
- out of pocket
- out of the frying pan
- out on a limb
- p's and q's
- pain and suffering
- panic button

- party pooper
- patter of little feet
- pass the sniff test
- pay through the nose
- peas in a pod
- perfect storm
- pig in a poke
- pillar of society
- plenty of fish in the sea
- poison pen
- poor as a church mouse
- poor excuse for
- pot calling the kettle black
- proud possessor
- put my/your foot down
- quick as a bunny
- quick and the dead
- radical chic
- rags to riches
- raining buckets
- raining cats and dogs
- rank and file
- read my lips
- red herring
- redheaded stepchild
- reign supreme
- remember the Alamo
- road to hell is paved with good intentions
- rob Peter to pay Paul
- rock and a hard place
- rocket science/scientist
- rope a dope

MAKING MONEY ONLINE AS A WRITING RETIREE

- run it up the flagpole
- running dog lackey
- safe than sorry
- salt of the earth
- save face
- scared stiff
- scared to death
- school's out
- screaming memes
- senses reel
- set the record straight
- shake a stick should of
- shoulder to the wheel
- shouldered his way
- shut your trap
- sigh of relief
- significant other
- silence is golden
- slept like a log
- small world
- snake in the grass
- snow job
- snug as a bug
- some of my best friends
- something the cat dragged in
- spade a spade
- spare the rod
- spitting image
- spring to life
- squeaky wheel gets the grease/oil
- start from scratch
- stick in the mud

- stick in your craw
- still waters run deep
- stop and smell the roses
- store bought
- stranger than fiction
- straw that broke the camel's back
- stubborn as a mule
- stuff that dreams are made of
- stuffed shirt
- take one for the team
- take the bull by the horns
- take the plunge
- takes one to know one
- talk turkey
- ten foot pole
- the earth moved
- the final analysis
- the real McCoy
- the same old story
- these things happen
- thick as thieves
- think outside of the box
- third time's the charm
- this day and age
- this point in time
- three strikes and you're out
- through the grapevine
- throw in the towel
- tiger by the tail
- till the fat lady sings
- time and time again
- time is of the essence

MAKING MONEY ONLINE AS A WRITING RETIREE

- tip of the iceberg
- 'tis the season
- to err is human
- to the best of my knowledge
- tongue-in-cheek
- too hot to handle
- touch of blarney
- tough as nails
- tough luck
- tough row to hoe
- traditional family values
- trials and tribulations
- tried and true
- trip down memory lane
- true blue
- turn your smile/frown upside-down
- twist of fate
- twists and turns
- two to tango
- under the gun
- under the same roof
- understated elegance
- unexpected twist
- until the cows come home
- up his sleeve
- up the creek
- up the wrong tree
- very real concern
- view with alarm
- wakeup call
- was my face red
- watch your tongue

- web of intrigue
- week of Sundays
- what a bummer
- what comes around, goes around
- what the cat dragged in
- what the dickens
- what the heck/hell
- what you see is what you get
- what's not to like
- wheeler-dealer
- when in doubt, punt
- when push comes to shove
- when rubber meets the road
- when the cat's away
- when the going gets tough, the tough get going
- who has everything
- whole ball of wax
- whole hog
- whole nine yards
- whole other story
- wild goose chase
- wild oats
- will wonders never cease
- wimp
- win friends and influence people
- win one for the Gipper
- winning is everything
- wisdom of the ages
- without benefit of clergy
- wolf at the door
- words fail

- work like a dog
- worst nightmare
- wrong side of the bed
- years young
- yellow journalism
- you are what you eat
- you can run, but you can't hide
- you know what they say
- young and foolish
- young and restless
- yuppie

Clichés are verbal exchanges that expand beyond borders. Everyone has heard them and is sure to have used at least one. While none of us uses *all* of these clichés *all* the time, each of us can recall one or more of them that we say unconsciously.

Specific *lingo* is common to different cultures. For instance, we communicate differently in Nevada than our counterparts do in Maine. The same is true for other townships. Language is territorial. It's clichéd, commanding its own insignificant corner of dialogue in the world.

The same is true for euphemisms or synonyms-- substituting visual description to identify character traits. For instance, instead of calling someone *stupid*, we would use sarcasms:

- *It takes him an hour to cook Minute Rice.*
- *All foam, no beer.*
- *The cheese slid off his cracker.*
- *One pickle short of a barrel*
- *One sandwich short of a picnic*
- *If you gave him a penny for his thoughts, you'd get change.*

Each of these descriptions tells the reader that the person being referred to is *"an ounce shy of a pound."* -- I just made that one up.

When thinking of serious writing, are these clichés and euphemisms helpful? Do they add character and variety to the work? Or do they reduce the manuscript to a mediocre effort?

Some English scholars believe clichés and slang discourse diminish writing's credentials, except where language enunciation identifies a character. Good writers instinctively know the difference.

The writer's character determines the tone of a piece, sarcasm at someone's expense. A cliché insults the essence of the person; place or thing it references. Whether this is a good or bad thing is for the reader and the writer to decide. However, it depends mostly on what message the writer wants to convey to readers.

It ultimately rests with the writer to decide whether their manuscript has a personality that requires the casual, loose feel of clichés.

For writers, the two principals are reading and writing-- not clichés, per se. If you read writers better than you-- and write everyday, your writing passion ultimately becomes your livelihood, your means of prosperity.

In the words of Ajay Ohri:

> "Write 50 words. That's a paragraph. Write 400 words. That's a page. Write 300 pages. That's a manuscript. Write every day. That's a habit. Edit and rewrite. That's how you get better. Spread your writing for people to comment. That's called feedback. Don't worry about rejection or publication. That's a writer. When not writing, read. Read from writers better than you. Read and perceive."

SECTION III
Words and Your Vocabulary
Writing Opportunities
Freelance Writing

Beautiful Words for Your Creative Writing Vocabulary That Represent Exquisiteness

1. **Amorphous**: indefinite, shapeless
2. **Azure**: blue color of a cloudless sky
3. **Beguile**: deceive
4. **Caprice**: impulse
5. **Cascade**: steep waterfall
6. **Cashmere**: fine, delicate wool
7. **Chrysalis**: protective covering
8. **Cinnamon**: an aromatic spice; its soft brown color
9. **Coalesce**: unite, or fuse around
10. **Crepuscular**: dim, or twilight
11. **Crystalline**: clear, or sparkling
12. **Desultory**: half-hearted, meandering
13. **Diaphanous**: gauzy
14. **Dulcet**: sweet
15. **Ebullient**: enthusiastic
16. **Effervescent**: bubbly
17. **Elision**: omission
18. **Enchanted**: charmed
19. **Encompass**: surround
20. **Enrapture**: delighted
21. **Ephemeral**: fleeting

22. **Epiphany**: revelation
23. **Epitome**: embodiment of the ideal
24. **Ethereal**: celestial, unworldly, immaterial
25. **Etiquette**: proper conduct
26. **Evanescent**: fleeting
27. **Evocative**: suggestive
28. **Exuberant**: abundant, unrestrained, outsize
29. **Felicity**: happiness, pleasantness
30. **Filament**: thread, strand
31. **Halcyon**: care-free
32. **Idyllic**: contentedly pleasing
33. **Incorporeal**: without form
34. **Incandescent**: glowing, radiant, brilliant, zealous
35. **Ineffable:** indescribable, unspeakable
36. **Inexorable**: relentless
37. **Insouciance**: nonchalance
38. **Iridescent**: luster
39. **Languid**: slow, listless
40. **Lassitude**: fatigue
41. **Lilt**: cheerful, or buoyant song or movement
42. **Lithe**: flexible, graceful
43. **Lullaby**: soothing song
44. **Luminescence**: dim chemical or organic light
45. **Mellifluous**: smooth, sweet

46. **Mist**: cloudy moisture, or similar literal or virtual obstacle
47. **Murmur**: soothing sound
48. **Myriad**: great number
49. **Nebulous**: indistinct
50. **Opulent**: ostentatious
51. **Penumbra**: shade, shroud, fringe
52. **Plethora**: abundance
53. **Quiescent**: peaceful
54. **Quintessential**: most purely representative of or typical
55. **Radiant**: glowing
56. **Redolent**: aromatic, evocative
57. **Resonant**: echoing, evocative
58. **Resplendent**: shining
59. **Rhapsodic**: intensely emotional
60. **Sapphire**: rich, deep bluish purple
61. **Scintilla**: trace
62. **Serendipitous**: chance
63. **Serene**: peaceful
64. **Somnolent**: drowsy, sleep inducing
65. **Sonorous**: loud, impressive, imposing
66. **Spherical**: ball-like, globular
67. **Sublime:** exalted, transcendent
68. **Succulent**: juicy, tasty, rich
69. **Suffuse**: flushed, full
70. **Susurration**: whispering
71. **Symphony**: harmonious assemblage

72. **Talisman**: charm, magical device
73. **Tessellated**: checkered in pattern
74. **Tranquility**: peacefulness
75. **Vestige**: trace
76. **Zenith**: highest point

Other Words for Your Creative Vocabulary That Represent Unpleasantness or Despair

1. **Acrimony**: rough, bitter manner
2. **Angst**: acute, or unspecific feeling of anxiety
3. **Brood**: alone in deep, or troubling thought
4. **Brusque**: rude, or peremptory shortness
5. **Cacophony**: confused noise
6. **Cataclysm**: flood, catastrophe, upheaval
7. **Caustic**: destroying, or chemical erosion
8. **Chafe**: irritate, abrade
9. **Coarse**: common, crude, rough, harsh
10. **Crestfallen**: dejected, dispirited, or discouraged
11. **Cynical**: distrustful, self-interested
12. **Decrepit**: worn-out, run-down
13. **Disgust:** aversion, distaste
14. **Dishevelled**: in disarray, or extremely disorderly
15. **Dissemble**: to deceive

16. **Grimace**: expression of disgust or pain
17. **Grotesque**: distorted, bizarre
18. harangue: rant
19. **Hirsute**: hairy
20. **Hoarse**: harsh, grating
21. **Leech:** parasite
22. **Maladroit:** clumsy
23. **Mediocre**: ordinary, of low quality
24. **Obstreperous**: noisy, unruly
25. **Rancid**: offensive, smelly
26. **Repugnant**: distasteful
27. **Repulsive**: disgusting
28. **Shriek**: sharp, screeching sound
29. **Shrill**: high-pitched sound
30. **Shun**: avoid, ostracize
31. **Slaughter**: butcher, carnage
32. **Unctuous**: smug, ingratiating
33. **Visceral**: crude, anatomically graphic

French Words and Phrases for Your Vain, Conceited or Romantic Character

With novels, there's something romantic about female characters visiting France and falling into bliss with a handsome French suitor. If you fancy using French words, look at these phrases and see if anything here is usable in your romance piece.

1. **affaire de Coeur**: love affair
2. **au contraire**: to the contrary
3. **au fait**: having practical knowledge of a thing
4. **autre temps, autres moeurs**: other times, other customs
5. **avec Plaisir**: with pleasure
6. **bête noire**: a thing especially disliked
7. **bon jour**: good day; hello
8. **bon soir**: good night
9. **bourgeoisie**: middle-class, materialistic
10. **c'est-à-dire**: that is to say
11. **c'est la vie**: such is life
12. **chacun à son goût**: each to his on taste
13. **coup de grâce**: death blow
14. **coûte que coûte**: cost what it cost
15. **dégagé**: without emotional ties

16. **de trop**: too much or too many
17. **dernier ressort**: last option
18. **Dieu avec nous**: God is with us
19. **Dieu défend le droit**: God defends the right
20. **en plein jour**: In full daylight; openly
21. **en rapport**: in sympathy
22. **fait accompli**: accomplished fact; finished act
23. **femme de chambre**: chambermaid
24. **fête champêtre:** outdoor festival
25. **gardez la foi:** keep the faith
26. **grand monde:** world at large; refined society
27. **honi soit qui mal y pense:** evil be with him who has evil thoughts
28. **ici on parle français:** French is spoken here
29. **jeu de mots:** play on words; a pun
30. **jeu d'esprit**: play of wit
31. **j'y suis, j'y reste**: here I am; here I stay
32. **le roi est mort, vive le roi:** The king is dead long live the king
33. **le style, c'est l'homme:** the style is the man
34. **mise en scène:** setting; environment; the stage
35. **mon ami:** my friend; my love (friendly)
36. **n'est ce pas?** - isn't that so?
37. **nom de guerre** - assumed name
38. **objet d'art** - object of art

39. **peu de chose** - a small matter
40. **pièce de résistance** - the primary event; main reason; principal meal
41. **pis aller** - last resort

42. **quand même** - nevertheless; nonetheless
43. **qui s'excuse, s'accuse** - he who excuses himself, accuses himself
44. **raison d'état** - for the good of the country
45. **raison d'être** - reason for being
46. **sans peur et sans reproche** - without fear, without reproach
47. **sans souci** - carefree
48. **tant mieux, tant pis** - so much the better, so much the worse
49. **voilà** - look or see

> *"If you can say it simply, you probably don't understand it."* -- Albert Einstein

Writing is not governed by a one-way technique that all writers employ, all the time. However, some preconditions are common to the profession, like noun and verb association, for example. And then there's correct spelling and basic grammar, along with sentence construction.

Benjamin N. Cardozo writes:

> *"There is an accuracy that defeats itself by the overemphasis of details. I often say that one must permit oneself, and quite advisedly and deliberately, a certain margin of misstatement."*

All writers must meet the foundational requisites when writing. However, as for style, tone and voice, these are subject to the writer's individuality, creative flow.

It is a particular style, voice or tone that causes a publisher to reject a manuscript. The storyline and the flow are perfect. The drawback is it's not the style of writing the publisher is looking for.

Major publications have guidelines that instruct the writer on what types of material they publish. Sometimes a publishing company is distinguished by genre, but not often; in which case, the writer sends out manuscripts and hopes for a favorable response.

Writers experience a lot of rejection. It's the trademark of a good writer. And because they couldn't bear repudiation, some gave up on writing as a profession.

Unfortunately, twenty-five percent of the rejection letters go out because the publisher never saw the submitted manuscript. Workers are at times overwhelmed by so many submissions that some manuscripts are tossed onto a rejection pile for the sake of productivity. Like "ratings", rejections are also overrated.

Thanks to independent publishing options, writers no longer have to send manuscripts to publishing houses. No more waiting months for an answer. Writers are finally in control of their own publishing.

It's possible to write, proofread, edit and publish your own books, with no lengthy contracts or upfront fees.

The fact that writers are in control of publishing their own books is an incentive to write, polish and submit their best work.

Paying Writing Opportunities for the Retiree

Writers come in variety. Not all of them are novelists or academic writers. Freelance markets account for seventy-eight percent of the writing community.

Freelance writing is one of the best ways to earn money from home. No special training is required, though having expertise is sometimes a requisite. You don't necessarily need a personal website to do it. While there are many opportunities in the writing market to go around, competition is fierce.

If you can write well enough, all you need is a word processor (computer program such as Microsoft Word). With Internet access, you can communicate instantly with publications you write for. They can send email notifications and remove weeks of postal wait time.

Lastly, as a well-written writer, you have all the creative ability you need to produce quality publication pieces, if freelancing is what you prefer.

Freelance writing appeals to retirees because the job is workable literally from anywhere--even while traveling. There is no clock to punch; therefore, no performance pressure. You can write when and where you want.

The first batch of listings represents blog-posting jobs. Each site typically posts writing guidelines to help writers submit work within the site's specifications.

Here's a list of writing opportunities and the amount they pay to help you get started. Sites and payment information referenced below reflect the status as of 2016. (*Particulars might have adjusted up or down by the time you read this information*)

- **Freelance Mom** pays from $75 up to $100 for well-written articles relevant to its platform. Visit the site for complete guidelines and article posting information: www.freelancemom.com/guest-post-guidelines.

- **Writers Weekly** pays $60 for a 600-word piece. Visit writersweekly.com for more details and complete guidelines.

- **Wealthy Web Writer** pays from $100 to $300, depending on the assignment. Get in-depth info at www.wealthywebwriter.com.

- **Metro Parent** (for southeast Michigan) pays between $35 and $350. If you're a writer living in the Michigan area, this is worth a nod. Visit www.metroparent.com.

- **Survival Life** is all about submitting articles and video survival courses that pay up to $2000. www.survivallife.com/contribute.

- **The Barefoot Writer** pays anywhere from $100 to $300 for accepted submissions. There are no guidelines listed; however, you can contact them via their online form, postal delivery or by phone at 866-879-2924 or 561-278-5557. Their website address is www.thebarefootwriter.com.

- **Stork Guide** is a site all about babies, toddlers and other *'baby'* relevance. The current pay rate is a flat $50 fee. This would be an interesting supplemental undertaking for this genre. The website address: www.storkguide.com/write-for-us

- **IWA Wine Blog** is strictly for wine lovers. It's the only type of blog posts they accept. They currently pay $50 per accepted article. blog.iwawine.com/iwa-contributor-guidelines.

A note on guest blogging:

At the risk of adding scepticism to the mix of opportunity, I must warn you of the other side of taking the guest blogging *submit-for-pay* route. It may not be all that.

There are reported instances where the writer's work gets rejected, but the site rewrites the content, using the submitted idea anyway.

If you decide to guest blog for an online publication, make sure it's reputable. Check with the BBB (Better Business Bureau) to see if they have a "reputation" *prior to* submitting your work. Post questions about a site you're considering on message boards and wait to see what the replies are.

On the other hand, there are those who *do* earn money from guest blogging. Vigilance is a needed virtue for this industry.

Having said all that, I view blogging as a self-contained effort, not a pay-to-post opportunity.

What I mean is you will earn more money hosting your own blog, providing a service that people need or want to read about. You will be a couple of years generating revenue from it, unless you already have a marketing affiliation that you can carry over.

Having and cultivating your own blog serves you better long term. Guest blogging is short-term uncertainty.

Freelance Writing Prospects that Pay Well

If you're a retiree and writing is your cup of tea, one or more of the listings in this book will appeal to you.

I mention retirees simply because this book caters to that community. It references how retirees or those over 50 can earn money writing. However, the book is not limited to a "retiree" audience. You will read something useful for you, if you're a writer of any age.

Aside from that, I'm retired. And I know the value of *time*. Writing requires time, of which retirees have plenty.

Whereas, working individuals, with families to care for, typically don't have the *time* required to produce well-written, well-thought-out material. I said, "Typically." There's an exception to every rule.

I found these four online opportunities ideal for those who can successfully break through the submission process.

- **Eating Well** is a national food magazine, with an online presence, that focuses exclusively on eating healthy. They currently pay $1 per word. www.eatingwell.com/writers_guidelines.

- **Country Magazine** pays $250 for submissions that run a page or more and $25 for short pieces that run in their *'Just for Fun'* section. See www.country-magazine.com/contributor-guidelines.

- **Chicken Soup for the Soul** normally runs powerful true stories about ordinary people who have extraordinary experiences. Published poems pay $200 and $100 for devotionals. See www.chickensoup.co/story-submissions/story-guidelines.

- **Cuisine at Home** publishes articles that offer a unique way of solving a cooking problem, paying up to $100 for accepted and published material. They take only unique and useful submissions. www.cuisineathome.com/contact/tip.php

➢ I list more home business ideas in the *bonus section*.

Online Sites Writers Find Interesting

We can always use more information. While no one has all answers, we will always find what we need as we sift through the knowledge pool of relevant books.

Having key information puts you ahead of the rest. On the other hand, it's better not to know, than to know and disrespect the knowledge you find.

But I digress.

The good part is it will not prove too difficult, finding what you need. You know exactly what to look for and where. Books like this are in a category all their own.

Finding specialty information is easy. Sifting through them to find what you need is time consuming, but worth it.

You can find valuable writing resources online. Writing aids, word substitutions and aids to help build characters for your novel are nestled somewhere on the web.

Do you see yourself sorting through thousands of websites? Maybe you don't have to-- at least, not yet. Go through the sites I've listed. See if one or more of them suits your needs.

- ✓ Former literary agent with Curtis Brown Ltd., Nathan Bransford is the author of *How* to Write a Novel. His Internet presence, **blog.nathanbransford.com** is a site you should visit. It has plenty of inside-scoop treasure.

- ✓ **"Men with Pens"** is an excellent site and should definitely be among the ones you frequent. Copywriting is their writing focus, still you will come away inspired. Some sites just make you feel good. This is one of them. **menwithpens.ca**

- ✓ **storyfix.com** is a general source for writing groups or book clubs seeking general training. Storyfix 2.0 offers coaching, public speaking and workshops for writing and book clubs that hosts seminars and such.

- ✓ On this site, a literary agent indulges in polite rants about queries, writers and the publishing industry. Believe me when I tell you, "This is a fantastic site." O the irony! **nelsonagency.com/pub-rants**

- ✓ Every writer is familiar with, or has at least, heard of *Writer's Digest*. Do yourself a favour and put **writersdigets.com** on your "favourites" list. A world of professional and valuable resources awaits you.

- ✓ **Mary Demuth** is a phenomenal woman and an author after my own heart. A true soul, who knows her path. Her website is both unique and inspiring, which gives it distinction. Visit **marydemuth.com**

- ✓ **writetodone.com** is a fantastic article site for writers, by editor-in-chief, Mary Jaksch. The site's main objective is to help writers build confidence by writing better.

- ✓ Editor, Alan Rinzler, hosts a fabulous blog for writers called *The Book Deal*. I recommend it. It's informative --and you know how I feel about information. Go to **alanrinzler.com** and have a look-see.

- ✓ Several of my fiction-writing friends contribute content to this site. They swear by the writers retreat. They're already packing for the one coming up in August. *Writer Unboxed* is anything but typical. Go ahead. Take the site tour. You'll love it. **writerunboxed.com**

- ✓ **Kidlit.com** originated as a resource site for fiction-writers of young adult and children's books. Though their reach is wider, writing kid's books is still its main genre. Go here: **kidlit.com**

BONUS SECTION

SOUND HOME BUSINESS IDEAS

Non-Internet Home Business Ideas

While the Internet is the most powerful invention since electricity, not everyone is cyber savvy, or wants to be.

The "mom and pop" business concept, the familiar storefront idea appeals to many budding entrepreneurs and retirees alike. However, that's not to say a storefront business can't hire a company to maintain a website for its marketing.

For the traditional businessperson, who prefers a physical location for their venture, the Internet does not have a monopoly on the long-established business model.

Here are thirty sound business ideas, of which you're sure to find one or more of interest.

1. **Day Care**: Parents who prefer their children learn in a home environment go into the childcare business. For them, a day care is the ideal business venture.

2. **Tutor**: Academically inclined persons of great patience, who love helping others achieve, will do well in this job capacity. Tutors charge by the hour or they can set a flat rate for a set amount of time. Either way, tutors are in great demand.

3. **Sign Maker**: This is for creative individuals with a knack for making beautiful and memorable marketing expressions. Sign designers can set their own fee.

4. **Bed and Breakfast**: This is great for large houses. My friend, Andi, inherited her father's huge estate home. After researching the idea and finding that the property was in a prime location for it, rather than sell it, she chose to do a quaint b & b that is doing well.

5. **Christmas Tree Sales**: This is a long-term planning effort for the rural property owner. The Balsam fir, which is the most traditional Christmas tree, requires seven years to grow into a five or six foot tree.

6. **Gift Basket & Specialty Shop**: A business like this can actually make a decent profit, provided there aren't any others in the area. Women cater to these shops regularly. Not to mention someone has a birthday or an anniversary every day. Choose a niche, micro target a market and launch.

7. **Personal Shopper**: People hire personal shoppers for many reasons. Not all of

them are incapacitated. Busy housewives and homemakers, corporate officials, bankers and other time consuming jobs require the services of personal shoppers. Build a trustworthy and dependable reputation, and you'll gain the business.

8. **Life Coach**: This is a popular endeavor among survivors of painful experiences or severe sickness and disease. They often build a life around helping others to survive life challenges and to heal and become whole again afterwards.

9. **Public Speaking**: This goes along with life experience and having something to offer of personal value that others want. Public speakers receive huge fees that include their travel expenses, food and hotel stays-- a field for the passionate and compassionate individual.

10. **Masseuse**: This endeavor requires some training, but is worth the time and effort. A masseuse earns anywhere from $75 to $200 an hour. You can even do a home office and service only a few select clients from your school P.T.O. or your church that you know and trust and still make out pretty good.

11. **Personal Trainer**: This is another occupation that usually requires formal training, as it deals with the physical body. You would have to know about the human anatomy, what restrictions an individual has and so forth. Trainers can set their own fee, depending on the client and what he or she wants. However, the trainer who goes to the client earns more money than the one who has a location.

12. **Jewelry Maker**: This works better if you already make jewelry as a hobby and are familiar with the mechanics of it. Custom jewelry is popular among the wealthy; and it brings in a hefty bounty. Not to mention you can have your shop in your home. No extra overhead expense.

13. **Upholsterer**: You could say this is one of the "evergreen" businesses. A couple of upholsterers in my area do well in this profession. They do a lot of restoration on old pieces that have sentimental value to the client. Some upholsterers also build furniture-- giving them the full-service benefit of the trade.

14. **Moving Service**: Most people who are moving don't care much for lifting heavy items. They would rather hire someone to do it. You can limit yourself to local,

across-town jobs; or to the next town. It's a good fit for those who are called to do these jobs anyway, because you have a large-sized truck. Why not get paid for it?

15. **Photographer**: Earning an income from this work is done in a number of ways. You can specialize in one area, like weddings. Or there are other niches like birthdays, family portraits, graduations, anniversaries and other occasions. The opportunities are limitless.

16. **Interior Designer**: For the lover of color and creativity, this is a fantastic career or even a part-time income supplement. This is a lucrative occupation that brings a perpetual flow of word-of-mouth business.

17. **Carpet Cleaner**: This requires knowing how to work with all kinds of carpet materials, such as wool blends and synthetics. You can leave the cleaning of specific to family heirloom restorations or antique carpets to the field experts and do basic cleanings.

18. **Landscaper**: Landscaping is basically a seasonal vocation that requires pre-scheduling because of the business rush

that accompanies spring and summer. If you train a large crew, you could cover two or more jobs at a time, monitoring each one throughout the day.

19. **Handyman**: A handyman is just that. He possesses many skills, and he does all of them well. This is not the "jack of all trades and master of none". A handyman's work quality can often replace a licensed plumber, painter or carpenter. And he can make a sizable income in the process.

20. **Housesitting**: Many retired couples, who love to travel, can see the world with the assurance that their home is protected against violation. Housesitting comes with many luxuries, one being a hefty fee for your services.

21. **Pet Sitter**: If you love pets, that's mostly all you need to do this job. Of course, you'll know something about different breeds of dogs, their mannerisms and what they need, in terms of care. Pet owners usually have to pay an exorbitant fee for the vet to house their pets when they have to be away from them for extended periods. They won't mind paying this fee to an individual who can

provide individual attention to their pet's needs.

22. **Pet Groomer**: Animal grooming is another great for the pet lover. Some groomers offer a dual service that includes sitting-- or vice versa. On the other hand, groomers and sitters often like to do one or the other; but find that combining the two is more lucrative. And since sitters have the pets for days at a time, grooming is usually a necessary chore. Why not get paid for it?

23. **Delivery Service**: This job offers ease to busy schedules by delivering groceries, dry cleaning, party supplies, appliances or whatever a customer has purchased. These services are popular in large and small cities alike.

24. **Catering:** Food, festivity and family. This is what catering usually consists of. Fine dining of exquisite menus is important during special functions. Establishing yourself as a unique caterer, who provides a combination of great food and service is worth it, if you're considering a catering business.

25. **Baker**: Bakers are always in demand for weddings, anniversaries, birthdays,

school activities and general events that require baked goods. Homemade rolls, cakes and pastries are especially popular around Thanksgiving and Christmas. This would be more of a seasonal flow of steady work. A great part-time job for the person who loves to bake.

26. **Auto Detailing**: This will forever be a steady, good-paying job. Taking a dingy, cigar-smoked interior, a dusty, lackluster finish and turning it into a shiny, fresh-smelling and luxurious automobile is what an auto detailer lives for.

27. **Window Cleaner**: Businesses employ window-cleaning services to keep their panes streak and smudge free. Window cleaners are in demand and are paid well for their services. There are large industrial cleaning services that tower tall buildings; or the small business that services local storefronts in town.

28. **Tax Preparer**: This, of course, is seasonal work and requires knowledge of the ever changing tax system. You will likely have to work for a tax franchise to learn the business before branching out on your own. Fortunately enough, most tax preparation franchises offer seminars and course training to their new hires.

29. **Accountant**: First, decide what services you intend to offer. Will you offer involved high-level accounting to major corporations or high-profile individuals, or does offering simple bookkeeping to small businesses appeal to you more?

30. **Used Book Sales**: Get those boxes of books out of the attic and the garage. Build a business around them. Clean them up and get them ready for sale. Decide where you will have your used book store. It would be great to have a small storage-size structure that they fixed up with a cool retro personality. You can stand it about fifty feet behind his house, with a bench for sitting and reading nestled under some magnolia trees, near a trickling bird bath.

3 Businesses That Day-Job Workers Can Start

Many day-job workers aspire to being their own boss, but can't afford to leave their nine-to-five job yet. It's good business sense to have a safety net to catch you if one method fails.

Working a full-time job doesn't leave much time for anything else, aside from kids and household concerns. That's why these three side-business ideas fit so neatly into your current set of obligations.

They are not demanding; you can choose how much time to devote to them. And the amazingly cool thing is you can do all of these from the luxury of your own home on your own time-- or not.

- **eBooks** - Yes. Write a book on your area of expertise, for starters. Don't worry about your writing ability. There are many experts in various fields, who are not confident in their writing skills. But that's no longer a hinder. You can hire a ghostwriter or an editor to refine your work. After the book is ready, all you need to do is publish it. And that's not as hard as it once was. Amazon is the most popular and reliable of self-publishers out there.

- **Food** - This endeavour requires more time from your schedule and may not be ideal for the person with a day job. But you may be able to pull it off. This is one (if not the only) of the leading areas of business service that is necessary to human survival. The food industry is here for perpetuity. You would need to research food licensing requirements for your area before doing any actual work. Then you can look at the number of things to choose from: start a food truck to deliver lunches; grow and sell produce at local markets; deliver organic meals, to give you the picture.

- **Blogging** - for the computer junkie, who loves surfing and doing productive things online, blogging, can be profitable. A few bloggers have sold their websites to profitable magazines or news outlets. You'll need understanding of online marketing and how to drive people to your website. Advertising and affiliate marketing are valuable, as long as you don't bog your site down with annoying popups.

These three "spare-time" efforts can turn into viable moneymaking ventures for the person serious about earning extra residual income.

Ways and Means to Make Money Online

There are many Internet moneymaking ventures to choose from, and some of them are not ethically sound. When looking for online earning opportunities, the BBB (Better Business Bureau) is a good verifier in determining which ones are safe to associate with.

Despite the uncertainty of finding reputable online opportunities, there are tried-and-true entities, solid skill areas that are trustworthy and sound.

I sectioned these into areas of skill and interest, describing pros and cons where applicable:

Freelancing

Freelancing is something you can begin with zero up-front investment. You can easily earn a five-figure monthly income in a specialized and in-demand field. Nevertheless, the freelance market is fiercely competitive and is full of intense bidding wars that cause capable contractors to work for way less than what the work warrants.

In-demand Freelance Fields

Writing - articles, newsletters, blog posts, print books, ebooks, brochures, booklets, reports, white papers, advertising copy and press releases.

- **Graphic Design -** web design, print design, corporate identity, logos, vectors, infographics, videography, business card and letterhead design.

- **Internet Marketing -** SEO, PPC account management, social media, sales copywriting, web site conversion optimization, sales, email marketing, PowerPoint presentation, public relations, blogger outreach and guest posting services.

- **Customer Service -** Data entry, virtual assistance, customer service rep, web research, telephone customer service, accounting and transcription.

- **Translating -** Languages in demand are Chinese, Spanish, Brazilian Portuguese and Japanese. You can usually find work, no matter what language you speak-- as long as you're skilled and experienced.

- **Programming** - WordPress, HTML5, PP, Ruby on Rails, mobile apps, (WordPress dominates the web right now) WordPress themes, plugins and programming; ecommerce, Joomla and MySQL.

Affiliate Marketing

Affiliate marketing is a way to make money promoting someone else's product. Although selling your own product from your own site is more profitable, this is another option if you don't have a product to sell. On the other hand, due to competiveness, this earnings market is losing its steam.

Online Affiliate Opportunities

- **Clickbank** - could be the largest digital goods marketplace in the business. They paid out over two billion to their publishers and affiliates over the last decade. It costs nothing to start. All you need is a website or blog to display the ads. This is the place for new affiliates to test the venture and make up to 75%

per sale.

- **Amazon Associates** - As an Amazon Associate, you will make significantly less per product sold than you would with Clickbank; however, you can make a lot promoting Amazon products.

- **Commission Junction** - This is similar to Clickbank and a good place to find products to sell.

- **Bluehost** - You can make up to $65 per sale by promoting this reliable web-hosting provider.

- **Apple Affiliate Program** - Yes. You can make a hefty commission promoting Apple products like iTunes, Apps and any other digital product Apple sells.

- **HostGator** - Make up to $125 in commissions promoting web-hosting similar to Bluehost.

- **ebay** - while this program is quiet after years of buzz, it can still earn you some cash from popular niches such as electronics, high-tech items and rare collectibles.

Remember. It's good to promote the things you love. You attach your name to your online transactions and validations. Make sure you have faith in the product you're promoting.

Arts, Crafts & Sewn Items

Mass-produced items are usually of low quality and badly made, which makes them subject to recalls. Not to mention everyone you know has one identical to yours. People absolutely love unique keepsakes that are handmade. If you're creative that way, why not sell your creations online? Here are a few outlets to get you thinking:

- **Etsy** - here you get to create your own store and have it up for business in minutes. Probably one of the most popular marketplaces for selling handmade wares online.

- **Art Fire** - Is another fabulous marketplace and Etsy's main competitor.

- **Folksy** - this is the British version of Etsy.

- **Zazzle** - Clothing designers never had it so good! Sell your personal clothing designs here.

- **Café Press** - create a design; upload it for approval; if they like it, they'll buy it to place on mugs, t-shirts and posters.

- **Spread Shirt** - a wonderful place to sell unique, one-of-a-kind t-shirt designs.

Avoid "Content Writing Mills"

Stay away from content marketing sites like *Hubpages* and *Constant Content*. They give you topics to research and submit articles. You'll spend hours researching and writing a topic only to have these *content mills* glean your work right from under you-- under the guise of *rejection*.

Desperate writers eager to have their work compensated flock to these sites. They literally have their pick from thousands of articles. The writer, on the other hand, goes unsatisfied.

Video Marketing

This is a huge business opportunity. Many Internet marketers make full-time salaries doing videos for YouTube audiences. If you get a loyal following, you can literally drive traffic to any site you want-- affiliate offer or a personal domain. Here is a list of video-sharing sites:

- **YouTube** - a tight niche (web site tutorials, cooking, dating advice) with consistent updates can do well.

- **Vimeo** - A place to upload your videos and earn money from them.

- **AOL.on** - Show off your expertise by doing tutorial-based videos for a new audience.

- **Flixya** - After uploading your vids to YouTube, putting them on Flixya will expose you to an extra million viewers a month.

- **Metacafe** - is another popular video sharing site.

- **Instructables** - a popular tutorial site for how-to videos.

- **Camtasia Studio** - expensive screen capture software for those who like doing tutorials. Did I say *expensive*?

- **Screencast Matic** - simple and easy to use (cheaper) alternative to Camtasia.

Q & A (Expertise)

If you're an expert in a particular field, you can make some side cash by answering questions on Q & A sites. Some people seek out these Internet resources when they want answers.

- **Live Person** - you can make money answering questions. All you have to do is register as an expert and answer questions over live chat, via email or over the phone.

- **Just Answer** - said to be the most popular of its kind on the Internet. They pay you well, but you have to know what you're talking about. Persons with degrees or other trained credentials do well here.

- **WebAnswers**.com - is a fairly new and growing site that pays you to answer questions.

Get Paid to Write Family & Parenting Articles

1. Earn $100 for each article accepted by *A Fine Parent Magazine,* an online publication. Visit www.afineparent.com/write.

2. *Adoptive Families* is a publication dealing with all angles of the adoption process. If you're an adoptive parent, go for it. You'll negotiate your pay for this job. Guidelines: www.adoptivefamilies.com/about-us/writers-guidelines/

3. *Babble* is a Disney interactive site that pays $100 to $150 for parenting posts. Email them at submissions@babble.com and ask for submission guidelines.

4. $50 is not a bad reward for telling the truth about parenting. Visit *Lies About Parenting* for details on jobs and writers' guidelines. liesaboutparenting.com/about-page/write-for-us/

5. Pitch the editor at the New York Time's blog on parenting. *Well* pays $100. well.blogs.nytimes.com/category/family/?_r=0

6. If you write original parenting posts, *Scary Mommy* pays $100. Read guidelines here: www.scarymommy.com/write-for-scary-mommy/

Get Paid to Write Essays

1. **XO Jane** pays $50 for essays about beauty, fashion trends you tried and basic women-focused topics. They love receiving essays about crazy things that happened to you. www.xojane.com/page/xojane-pitching-guidelines

2. The *New York Times'* **Modern Love** column pays $300 for essays on personal accounts of relationships descriptive of *modern love*. www.nytimes.com/2010/12/21/fashion/howtosubmit_modernlove.html?_r=0

3. **Guideposts** magazine reportedly pays $250 for true stories about/by people who have attained a goal, overcome obstacles or learned valuable lessons through their faith. www.guideposts.org/writers-guidelines

4. **The Establishment** is an all-inclusive publication that will pay $125 for essays and reported stories that captivate. Visit www.theestablishment.co/pitchus/

5. **Cosmopolitan.com** pays $100 for essays of your college experience. Submit it here: www.surveymonkey.com/r/?sm=P%2bTI3

UALB1rlCBgvlYElag%3d%3d (The form is hosted by Survey Monkey).

6. **B. Michelle Pippin** pays $50 to $150 for business-related articles that focus on "hacks", or how to do something better. www.bmichellepippin.com/get-paid-to-share-your-expertise-with-us/

I Can't Afford to Give a Damn What You Think

"An idea that is not dangerous is unworthy of being called an idea at all." -- Oscar Wilde

Writing is a dangerous sport-- not for the reader, but for the writer. It's dangerous because a true writer is unconventional. Thinking without a box is madness to those inside the box. But that's what a genuine writer does. He thinks and writes without restraint-- outside the box.

Consider, for a moment, the "free writer" concept. Is it wrong for him to write freely the wisdoms of his soul? Are we a freethinking society that restricts expression of thought? Do we dare tell a man or woman what to write? Then what if they disobey?

Writing is the mirror in which the writer looks. He invites the reader to look into it as well. Each image is individual to the one looking. And maybe that's the problem.

We *say* we believe in freedom of speech. It sounds patriotic. We believe in it as long as it's not *too* freely spoken or written.

There's nothing more phenomenal than the word written unfettered and in truth. Only when

words are not owing to anyone do they render service, like a medicine, to the reader. Some people don't want to get well. Sickness can be contagious.

If someone disagrees with your writing, your book by saying something flippant and nasty, it's fair to say that person didn't like the taste of the medicine. A 1-star rating may be your lot. But this will always be the reality when you choose to write unrestrained.

Give me a sheet of paper and I'll begin to think. Hand me a pen or pencil, and I'll write a melody for your mind to sing.

Disagree with what I write, but leave the freedom to do it my way in tact. Express too much animosity and you reveal your true intention.

I will continue to write. In my sleep, I'm writing a passage for when I awake. I will continue to write unshackled by what you think of what I write.

I will write unafraid. Unabashed. Unparalleled. And I will read in the same manner. If you write books, I'll read your books. But a *rating* I will not give it. If your book is not worth the read, I simply won't recommend it. Ratings are over-rated.

If I ask people why they leave malicious notes, they would need a day to ponder. There's no reasonable explanation for spite. You could blame it on *wickedness*. What would that say about your state of being? We could say your upbringing is a contributor. And how old are you again?

Your plight is yours. Mine is mine. My difficulty drives me to write, to share, and to instruct. It's therapy for me. All three.

If you are of a bunch who seeks to tread down, like grass, a writer's work, apparently, your plight moves you to cruelty, to treachery and to bitterness.

How sad for you. How utterly sad. It is for this reason that I decided not to give a damn. To leave you in your stupor is the only reasonable action. After all, you're probably ten years my senior. That you don't do better by humanity is disturbing.

Nevertheless, I can't afford to give a damn when you challenge me. So I don't. On the other hand, the universe does.

SECTION IV
The End of This One

Writing This Book Did Me All the Good

I couldn't be happier. It was good therapy for me to write this book. Especially after receiving so many emails asking for more books like *"How to Make Money Online When You're Over 50"*. This book was born as a result.

The first volume came from an inspiration to help people see that being a retiree is a good thing. I felt compelled after hearing, as if for the first time, the hopelessness in people my age, as they talk about how "life is over" now that they've retired. "Wait a minute. We're the same age." I thought.

Immediately, I saw the need for the kind of book I was to write. There may be others out there. But none of them say what I say the way I say it. In the first book, I wanted to encourage retirees with a mini stimulus, showing them other options. I wanted to do it with a global voice. And I did.

Now that I've received emails asking for more, I know the message resonated. You want more. Meet the sister volume *"Making Money Online as a Writing Retiree Anyway: Despite 1-Star Reviews"*.

I'm gratified that the first mini volume touched you the way I intended. I'm honoured by your well wishes. I'm humbled by your praise. Because of you, I write with my soul. To give you words that work.

Other books by this author:

Teen Survival: Recognizing & Escaping Abusive Dating Relationships

Babies Having Babies: Girls Interrupted

Words to Grow By

From Healing to Wholeness: A Journey Worth Taking

A Journey in Verse

How to Make Money Online When You're Over 50

Website: peggyhatchetjames.com

Thank you for reading

www.ingramcontent.com/pod-product-compliance
Lightning Source LLC
Chambersburg PA
CBHW021433170526
45164CB00001B/218